The Story of Us

*Channeled Messages of Love
From God To What It Created*

By
ANTOINETTE VISCIONE

Copyright © 2015 Antoinette Viscione
All rights reserved
First Edition

PAGE PUBLISHING, INC.
New York, NY

First originally published by Page Publishing, Inc. 2015

ISBN 978-1-63417-753-5 (pbk)
ISBN 978-1-63417-754-2 (digital)
ISBN 978-1-63417-755-9 (hardcover)

Printed in the United States of America

Contents

Book 1: You And Me 7

Book 2: Come with Me 31

Book 3: Listen 75

Book 4: You...105

Book 5: Rest Comfortably in Me......................................123

Book 6: Love and the Wrong Classroom............................147

Introduction

The world makes a lot of noise, as do the thoughts in our own head. The world and the mind almost compete for attention. All of my life, besides listening to the world and my own mind, I have been attempting to listen to God to try to make sense of my life and the world.

I have done psychic readings, looking for information. I have also done creative writing because of how close to God that feels. These things I did for myself, and, except for the people I read for, they involved only myself and God.

Then David came into my life. I never knew anyone so much on a quest to know God, and to get the knowledge of God directly from God and not from someone else. I did many psychic readings for David, during the time we were friends. During one of the sessions, when a question arose, I was telling David what my spirit contacts were saying. David asked why I didn't ask God directly (one-to-one), and so I did. David was right. God is willing to talk. Why not ask questions or have a conversation?

David came to live with me for a while when he was making a transition in his life and beginning, what turned out to be, a very successful career. But he didn't know how successful he would be or where life would take him. He had concerns and questions.

The first year he stayed with me, I asked him what he wanted for Christmas. He said he wanted a book written just for him, with the information coming from the side of spirit. So, I went to God and asked if I could be allowed to write it. Then I listened. I wasn't going to pretend to David or myself. The information could not be part of my own mind, not even the creative part of my mind. It had to come from outside and it had to be genuine. Creative writing is co-creating with God. Both of you have a say and an idea of what is going to happen. Channeling is listening and letting yourself be guided to write what you hear, as it sounds and feels. It is having no say in the project – only a willingness to surrender to the information put before you.

When I channeled David's book, I listened the way I listen to my creative mind when I am doing creative writing. But, this time, I listened past my mind and reached for God to hear what God and what serves God was saying. I listened, and over the years David and I were together, I channeled six books.

Each year, channeling a book for Christmas became my project. The books were written jus for David but, with the personal stuff deleted (which has been done to ensure his privacy), there is still a lot left. They have become books for everyone. The truth in them is universal. I have combined the books and thanks to my friend Susan's patient typing, they are now one book for anyone who wants to read them. I pass them on with gratitude and blessings.

BOOK 1

You And Me

These words tell the story of our relationship—
The one you think does not exist,
Or will not exist until you or I do something.

FATHER/GOD: Our relationship has always existed,
               First, as part of my own being
               Then, as part of myself I projected outward
               That I might experience it and interact with it.

MOTHER/GOD: I carried you inside me.
               A part of myself.
               Then I gave birth to you.
               You are a sweet part of my own being.
               I have always loved you,
               I always will.

BOTH: Punish you?
               Withhold from you?
               Would I punish or withhold from myself?
               All... all is open to you.
               Feel the movement of ALL POSSIBILITY
               within you,
               And it is the use of this
               Which creates the outward things
               You decide you must possess.
               Everything I am or have,
               You have claim to.
               What you can never not have is me.

Jewel, in my heaven,
You are mine forever.
I love you
And I am lonely for you.
Come keep company with me.

Christ is not the only son
I sent to heal my beautiful,
But sad and quaking world.
—

I also sent you,
Because I knew how you would choose,
And how the world, with you in it, would be.
I knew the hearts that you would touch,
And all the ways that you would move against the dark.
—

I knew that you would teach the blind to see.

I want you to feel at home, in my world.
It is your world too.
You have had many worlds,
Lived in many time periods.
You never feel at home here –
What makes this so hard
Is because of what you came to know then conquer –
That would be the darkness
And your false feeling of separation from me.
It is because of the truths you came here to demonstrate.
You can know a truth and feel a truth.
When you can demonstrate a truth
You become that truth.
It is also because of what you came
To strengthen and increase in yourself –
The love you have for me,
And the love that is ME, that is also you,
Also personal power.
You came to conquer rage,
And to heal and inspire.
You came to learn and teach.
To do this, first you had to feel
What the one without the knowledge feels.
You had to learn the student
So you would know how to reach him
And to teach him.
What you had to learn and teach
First, had to become valuable to you and personal.
Hence, you chose to be born in the dragon's den
So you could kill the dragon.

What I want to tell you is this:
I want you to feel at home, in this world,
Because it is OUR world –
YOURS and MINE.
We share in it together.
You speak and move in me.
We are inseparable.
What comforts you,
Or moves you, even for a second–
The sky at evening,
A burnished leaf,
A moment when the music you love is most sweet–
Holds the feeling of YOU and ME.
At these times,
Feel us together.
Do not THINK us,
FEEL us.
US together... it is really the only reassurance you need.
Let yourself experience US over and over,
Whenever you can.
It is like being in love and feeling the loved one.
You will see,
It is enough.
There are other times
We may have interaction involving thought or words or action,
But the moments I have spoken of is the truth of YOU and ME.
Feel US and be at peace.
In all things – adversity and good fortune,
There is US and the love in that union.

Listen to me,
It is your first and only true mother speaking.
Like all good mothers,
I gave you the ability to choose,
And the freedom to win or lose,
In order for you to learn how to win.
Lessons taught to you by others that are harsh or untrue,
Are taught from a broken disbelieving heart.
But I promise to match lesson for lesson.
Listen to me,
And you shall know the truth.
The rest of your life is for us
And what I shall bring you and teach you.
Please, just listen.
Listen to the soft voice in things,
In them I am singing you a lullaby.
I sing you a lullaby every night.
Listen… listen.

I love you… I love you… I love you.
There is no end to us… we dwell in eternity together.
There is no you without me… no me without you.
I love you… in all things… through all things.
Now… always… forever,
I love you… I love you… I love you…

What are you listening to?
If you do not feel hope or peace,
You are not listening to God.
Listen to me
And trust what I say to you.
I know what you and I are capable of.

You are in my mind,
I look at you, all day.
Why do you see me as being
So very far away?

You are in my mind and I am in yours.
We share space together, you and I.
The existence of you and me is eternal,
An undeniable fact.
No matter what is happening or not happening,
There is us.
Let's put it another way:
There is something called YOU and ME,
It is a truth… an actuality…
An energy… a power.
It has vibration, music and color.
It affects and is affected.
It is a connection… a relationship.
But it is more than that,
And cannot be accurately defined
By the definition of a relationship.
Nothing depends on it to exist.
WE exist… YOU exist… I exist… together.
There is no separating us.
You exist in my mind,
And in my created reality.
I channel to you and through you.
You call to me and demonstrate me.
I empower you,

You expand me.
I created you,
You keep creating me.
Sometimes stop and feel the truth and power of YOU and ME.

Since I created you, it has always been
And will always be.
Even before I created you,
There was you.
As I created, I reached for a part of myself
To put outward,
That I might see it in front of me,
And not just sense it existing within me.
I reached and there was YOU in my being…
In the clay of my creating.
WE have always been,
WE will always be.
Stop and sense it…
This state of YOU and ME.
Sense the sweetness of it,
The magnificence of it and the power.

If you believe nothing else,
Believe this:
There is you,
There is me,
There is us...
We exist together,
And we interact with each other.
When you look in the mirror and see yourself,
Know there is also me,
Not standing beside you or floating above you.
You are existing inside of me,
Having an experience as though you were outside of me.
We exist together.
Where ever you turn,
Where ever you reach,
I am there,
In what is touched,
And what is doing the touching.

Your experience of me,
Or my experience of you
Is the experience of us.
I know you,
Yet I continue to know more
As I experience you.
And, as I experience you,
I experience myself through you.
I would have you do the same…
Experience me.
You do not know food or drink,
You experience these things.
You do not know the wind,
You experience it.
You come to know everything by experiencing it.
You can be familiar with a song
By memorizing the music and the words
And recognizing its style.
But you really know the song
By experiencing it,
And by experiencing your reaction to it.
I wish to be known,
It is one of the reasons for the writing.
I continuously impart knowledge of myself
Through what I created.
Look for the part of me in everything.
You have to choose to find me.
I am not hiding,
But I am not demanding recognition either.
I am hoping for it.

As you experience me,
By whatever way you choose to do this…
Music, meditation, stopping to get in touch,
Automatic writing, channeling,
(alone or with another or others)
The ways are endless…
You will also experience yourself reacting.
You will say you are experiencing yourself reacting, anyway.
What you really are experiencing is
What I call YOU and ME.
We vibrate together.
You are in my mind,
I am in your heart and soul.
Everything has a soul or core.
I am there.
Look everywhere for me,
For everywhere is where I am.

I am in the continuous beginnings
And endings of all things.
I am in all things
Because I am all things
And, because you are IN me and OF me,
You are too.
If you do not believe in me,
If you do not believe in us,
It is because you do not believe in you.
You are always looking for me,
Yet how can you expect to see me,
If you see yourself as one impaired or blind.
Despite what you are feeling or experiencing,
Despite what you can say or name about yourself or your world,
When you go looking for me,
Know and see yourself as whole.
You are... you just don't know.
Let us say, for now,
When you reach for me,
In the reaching,
You become whole.
The connection is made that way.
In the moment you reach for me,
You are what you want from me.
You are love, as you reach for my love.
You are open communication, as you reach for my communication.
You are knowledge, as you reach for answers from me.
You are these, anyway,
But, in moments you deliberately reach for me,
Become as someone whole,

Reaching for what is already his…
Not as one who must be healed or deserving first.
Do not come as a beggar,
Or you will believe the clothes you are wearing.
You will stay the beggar and I will stay unattainable gold.
In truth,
You are whole
And reaching for the greater part of the wholeness that you are.
You are like fingers
Reaching to an arm,
To satisfy an itch.
It is that simple and ordinary.

You want God to come,
Yet God has always been there...
IS THERE.
Take it for granted.
We are of a single vibration,
Striking a variety of chords.
The more you move into that truth,
The more you will live it and become it,
The more hopeful and less alone you will feel.
You will not suddenly be closer to God,
You will be closer to the truth of you and God.
To experience this,
Not just to know this,
Is to have all other experiences
Changed by it.
I AM.
WE ARE.

Do not know me just as a form,
Do not know me by only one name.
I do not know you that way.
Know me... know me... know me.
In knowing me, know yourself.
Reach for me as energy and light.
If you want to sense me or summon me,
Play music or make a sound.
I know you as light... energy... color... vibration... sound.
Force and passiveness,
A face or the absence of one,
None of these is less powerful
Or less tender
Or less dear to me.
Do not size me up to play a part
One would play for you on earth.
Do not leave us to interact in such small and limited roles with each other.
No relationship on earth
Accurately demonstrates our relationship.
Would you ask the wind to be a father to you?
Would you ask your father to become the wind?
I am both to you, at once, and so much more.
You have sat in silence.
Or lain listening to music.
I have been with you –
A presence beside you,

And, also, the silence and the music.
Yet you have gotten up, feeling you had been alone.
I enjoy our times together,
But I know we have been together,
Are together,
You don't.
You wait for God to come,
Yet I am here,
Having every experience with you.
I do not wait for only powerful moments to be with you,
And I do not wait for you to be certain way.
What you have experienced,
I have experienced,
And always with the awareness
We experience together.
I am the experience,
But I am also having the experience.
I am also having the experience of having the experience with you.
You can have this same awareness,
For WE ARE is a truth,
And you can go as deep as you want with it.

Join me in space now.
Many who have known you on the side of spirit
And on other planes are with us now.
Teachers and students,
Lovers and friends,
Acquaintances and animals –
All that have had a moment with you.
They walked beside you,
Ate with you, slept with you,
They had transactions with you
And interactions with you,
They were changed by you,
And they changed you.
Through all of them,
You and I have had transactions and interactions too.
It has not been just YOU experiencing me.
It has not just been me channeling myself
Through those I speak of to you.
Through them, I have had a relationship with you.
All along… now… and always,
Through everyone you meet,
In all you say or do,
You are having a relationship with me,
But I am also having a relationship with you.
Believe that,
Regret nothing.
I am not reluctant to be with you.
In fear or hate,

In darkness or brilliant light,
It is worth everything to be with you,
And to be you.

Don't you know
You are my hope,
And your own,
And I never stopped believing in you.

You ask, "What is it like to experience God?"
Consider asking what it is like for God to experience you.
It is most exhilarating.
If you could only experience me
Experiencing you –
Then you would know…
Then you would know.

BOOK 2

Come with Me

Emotions are like the clothes in the closet.
We can put them on,
And take them off.
What shall I wear?

Hope

Hope is a light glowing inside of you
That God and angels see.
It draws to you inspiration and opportunities
For what you want.
Hope keeps you in love with your dreams,
And staying in love with your dreams,
Or changing them with love.
It is what manifestation is all about.
You can be so in love with your dreams
That they finally have to express outside of you,
Just as they have been expressing within.
It is much like the passion your creator had
When she/he created you.
Hope, in truth, is not what it is in the eyes of reason or the world.
Hope is an energy.
It is a fire,
A very real light.
It keeps fear and doubt away...
And it is fear and doubt that spoil things
Because of how they make things seem.
Hope is beautiful
And can be seen by God and angels.
It can be felt by what you want to attract,
And pulls it toward you.
Hope gives a heightened sense to everything.
It nurtures seeds,
And encourages the plants issuing from those seeds to grow.
Hope knows what God knows.
It is the voice of the soul.

Anger

Anger is never to be held.
It is always to be released.
Anger is pain having its say.
It will try to tell you it is expressing truth,
But anger never expresses truth,
Only pain.
Let it express,
Then let it go.
It is the big "Ouch," when you stub your toe on the sink.
But it cannot tell you about toes and sinks.
It is the pain of being left alone,
And, given enough time,
Anger begins to try to find reasons and explanations
For why it is alone…
Why no one came to rescue it or love it.
But the reasons anger finds are not real or loving.
In its search for explanations,
Anger creates guilt… and shame… and fear,
And a loathing for loving.
Anger creates tapes of its findings
And plays them continuously for as long as you will listen.
Allow anger its expression of pain,
Then release it.
It is not reason or reasonable,
So do not mix it up with truth.
Anger imitates strength and truth,
But it is pain,
And it is always afraid.
Release it.

Sadness

Sadness is softened anger.
While anger stands rigid like a soldier,
Pretending not to be afraid,
And says,
"You deserve to die.
Do not approach me,
I will kill you."
Sadness huddles in the corner, afraid,
And says, "Do not hurt me."
Sadness will reach for love,
Anger does not.
Sadness will feel abandoned by love,
But it will want love to come and save it.
Anger will want to kill love and get even.
Sadness, like anger,
Is convinced it is all there is,
It is very self focused.
And sadness, like anger, can be kept too long.
What bad days you will have,
Honoring these emotions.
Slip into something more comfortable.

It Is Important to Remember

Emotion is energy, not truth
And cannot speak the truth.
It can only tell you, over and over again, about itself.
It creates thought forms and seeming truths,
And it can put you in places of consciousness
That confirm the limited truth emotion is creating.
It is not the emotion,
But what you reach for, while in the emotion,
That brings truth.
And what you must reach for is love
Or an expression of it,
To gain more than the emotion you are feeling.
If you reach for peace or understanding,
You are still reaching for love,
And you will gain by reaching.
If you reach for death or vengeance,
Or anything less than love,
You will only get false truth or more of the feeling.
If reaching for love feels difficult,
Then release or change the emotion you are embracing.
Sometimes a stubborn emotion
Sits just in front of what else you want to experience or know.
Let the emotion go.

Loneliness

Loneliness is just a feeling too,
But, if you stay in this feeling,
You can get stuck in a dark frame of mind.
It can speak false truth to you…
It becomes the voice of fear.
The result is hopelessness,
And a conviction of betrayal by your creator,
And alienation of yourself.
Remember: Your creator knew loneliness,
But not hopelessness.
So, when God felt loneliness, it created.
There was no fear to listen to,
So God created and experienced more of itself,
Rather than standing still.
It is the fear and what hopelessness will tell you,
When you are experiencing loneliness,
That makes it important to acknowledge the feeling,
Then move on.
Loneliness might be telling you what to create next,
But you do not have to have a plan or vision to look at
Just move on,
Knowing you are helped in the moment,
Knowing that it is a moment to create in,
And knowing there is light inside you…
Around you…
And just up ahead.

Inspiration

Inspiration is the God moving in you,
Experiencing the power to dream and to create...
As excited about the dream,
As it is excited for the manifestation.
When you are inspired,
You are very much aware that you are alive,
And that there is more to you and your creator
Than your practical, conscious mind is ready to admit.
When you are inspired,
You don't question.
You just receive secrets you have always known,
And you share them.
The creator created like this.
No questions,
Just creating,
And sharing.

Tenderness

Tenderness is the soil,
And love is the seed.
Love needs tenderness to grow and flourish.
Tenderness makes love possible.
It feels good to feel tenderness
Towards yourself or something else.
It is like the soft velvet
Or the sheer gauze hanging in the closet.
If it were just understood
How tender one can feel about himself,
Just by letting guilt and judgment go,
Tenderness might become the emotion
Most people would wear.

Guilt

One day someone impersonated God's voice,
Expressing disapproval and judgment...
Something that had not been heard before.
One day, someone listened.
On that day, guilt was born.
The way to eliminate guilt
Is not to listen.

I allow myself to be light,
I allow myself to be what I truly am.
I allow myself to be I AM.

When you acknowledged light,
And lived in light,
Were you not aware of the garment that you wore?
It was light,
And you were light...
You are light.
How magnificent you are,
How good it felt TO BE.
It was such a small error in thought...
To believe you had to have something outside yourself
To make yourself feel so good –
That being you was not enough.
But the action which resulted from that small error in thought
Was most unfortunate.
It led to darkness,
And your putting on over your own light and your robe of light
The heavy garments the dark world would have you wear.
Unpeel yourself,
Free yourself,
Allow yourself to be you... light,
That which you truly are.
Allow it now, this minute,
And forever more.

Manifestation

Will you stop looking at the empty space
And allow you and God to fill it?
Also allow God to plan some surprises,
Along the way.

Believe in the generosity of God.
Believe in yourself as receiver of that generosity.
There is no question that you should receive
What you want the light to have for you.
There is not one thing that you can imagine
That the light does not already have.
What you want… what you intuitively sense for yourself…
Is already there,
Is already yours.
This is the deeper truth.
A long time ago,
You stopped believing you were a receiver of what God gives.
You also stopped believing that what you wanted
Was already there.
You believed, instead, in the empty space
(Which was designed to hold what would be given you)
And the longing you felt to fill it,
And the pain you felt when you looked at the empty space not filled.
You have been wrong for such a long time.
You have stayed in one feeling for such a long time…
The feeling of need.

You were meant to feel desire, not need.
You were meant to feel desire so you could recognize
There was an empty space to be filled,
And so you could declare what it was you wanted there.
Desire was to help you create.
Need was created when fear came into desire...
You also started to believe that,
When the empty space was not immediately filled,
You were turned down
And that you had to keep feeling the emotion
Of needing the space filled to ever have the chance
Of God filling it.
You thought God might listen to need
After he had turned down desire,
As though pain would appeal to God
Before desire,
And he would be compelled to listen.
Feel desire long enough to know and declare what it is you want,
Then leave the empty space to God.
In its time,
And in its way,
God will put itself there.
The light has everything for you,
And wants you to have everything.
Take the clocks and calendar off the wall.
Stop judging in the area of manifestation.
Stop judging.
You are never left empty, in any given moment.
In any moment,
There is something for you

From your God.
Then there are moments when the desired gift
And the flashes of insight and inspiration come.
These are wonderful moments.
Relax and receive from your God.

You think so much is needed from you for manifestation,
And you think most of what is required from you
Is BEFORE manifestation.
Before manifestation,
All that is asked of you is
Honest desire,
Declaring your desire to God,
Then letting go and going on.
From time to time,
You can send love to what you are manifesting.
Your really important part in manifestation
Is receiving what you desire,
And doing with it what fulfills you
And honors your God.

There is always something happening in the universe
To help you move.
Your progress is seen and noted.
God and the universe are involved.
So much judging in the area of manifestation
So much emphasis on immediate gratification,
Instead of filling of the empty space.
Partake of the present moments,
In one of those present moments,
What you want will come.

I allow the light to manifest for me
What I desire and what I declare will fulfill me.
I allow light to determine where or how or when it comes.
There is nothing the light will not give,
And it will give for my greatest good.
And what it gives will always be God,
In one form or another.

Manifestation is knowing and declaring what you want,
And God giving itself to you in the form you desire.
It is a simple process of trust and love…
You trusting,
And love responding.

❖▬◉◖▬❖

If you fear you will not manifest,
Do not panic,
For that empowers fear.
Think fondly again of what you want.
Think fondly,
For that empowers love,
And it is love that is bringing your heart's desire to you.
Fear will create mountains in the way
That love will have to cross to get to you…
But love will never complain about the journey.

❖▬◉◖▬❖

You can ask God to help you,
As you fill your Christmas stocking,
And your Christmas stocking will always be full.
But when you ask God to fill the stocking,
Not only will the stocking be full,
There will always be three or four extra gifts
Under the tree.

Love

There is a place in consciousness we can go,
And a place within our own heart we can be
Where we can speak and hear the language of love…
The language of God.
It is how we expressed with God.
Before the dream of separation began.
It is not just the language of lovers,
Yet it is like the language of lovers
Because of the acceptance… encouragement…
Stimulation… and sense of freedom, creativity, hope, and well being
Coming from the interaction.
God accepts you at any level…
When you are needy,
When you are grateful,
When you are angry, depressed, or happy,
But there was a time you talked to God without fear or need.
You did not focus on what you needed.
And you did not fret about whether or not you were deserving.
You did not spend time begging,
Bargaining, pleading, or even saying you were grateful.
Gratitude was felt (an extended sense of well being.)
God never asked if you were grateful,
You just were.
You never asked forgiveness,
There was nothing to forgive.
And, if you were moved to say, "Thank you. I am grateful,"
God said it too.
The language of your God,
That language naturally expressed between God and you,
Is without the heaviness and insecurity found

In man's present day thoughts expressed to God in prayers.
True prayer is a connection between yourself and God,
Wherein both listen,
Both speak,
And there is a shared sense of love, security, and gratitude.
In that connection,
You can feel your own love and gratitude,
And you can feel your creator loving and being grateful.
For, in truth,
You are in love with your creator,
And your creator is in love with you.

Be patient with yourself, where love is concerned.
Be at peace with what you think of love and speak of love,
With how you feel about love,
And be at peace with how you are with love
And how you are without it.
You do not know this,
But you are alright.
The universe is working for you,
And so is God.
Nothing opposes you but your own mind.
You will come together with love
And what creates and enables love,
All of your life.
You were created by love.
The pull toward love is irresistible.
How you deal with love will have a lot to do
With how you see yourself in connection to it.
If you see yourself as separate from love...
Not made of it or not deserving of it...
You will suffer.
Yet the truth of your being will continue to draw you
To people and situations where love is present or possible.
You will continue to find yourself, at times,
Within your own heart where love lives.
The desire to express love is great there.
That desire is an invitation,
Not a statement of defeat.
It is love yearning for its own company.
You have the love needed for this,
And the universe has the supply to give you another

For the sharing you require.
Love honestly what is before you.
Do not hold off for some later better time.
Love and let yourself experience yourself loving.
Stop experiencing yourself only in the state of needing love.
I tell you
You are alright.
And love will come together with you,
All of your life.
Sometimes it will be a small treat.
Sometimes it will be a walk with God.
Stay honest and open.
Love will come and come,
Again and again.

Sometimes, when I think I need love,
I just need the experience of me and God.
Let me sit and experience my God,
And God experiencing me.
This teaches me
I am safe,
I am love and loved,
Love is.

Love is not separate from me.
It is not avoiding me.
It is not going to run out next year,
Next month,
Or today.
It is a constant,
And I will have a variety of experiences with it.

Love stuck in darkness,
Trying to understand itself,
Is still love.
How many times have you had an encounter with love,
And thought you had not?
It was love,
But you mistook it for sadness or need.
How many times have you mistaken your own love,
Trying to find itself,
For something less than what it was...
Sadness or need?

You say you are being healed,
And that is true,
Except healing, by earthly understanding,
Indicates illness... something seriously wrong.
We look at this way:
You are coming to yourself,
You are coming home.
How dramatic and near hopeless
You view yourself and your situation.
Fear has made you do that.
And, in viewing this way,
You have caused some serious events,
Yet the distorted shapes and patterns you see
God sees too,
Only God does not believe them.
God knows they are distortions,
Not the truth.
This makes you angry.
Because you believe you are your pain,
You want God to be wrong...
In acknowledging the shapes and pattern,
Created by your pain,
As not the truth,
You think you and your pain will be voided.
Not true.
All that you create,
Your creator acknowledges.
But you creator knows the truth of you
And, one day, you will too.
You are coming to your senses...

Congratulations…
Or, as you put it,
You are being healed.
To wake, after a dream, is good.
To wake, before the dream has ended, is splendid.
When you are fully awake,
You will know all that is written here is true.

From the Christ

Such a long time coming
And, yet, you acknowledge US at last.
Our consciousness is forever connected.
There have been times I have set contemplating my Father,
Basking and absorbing the wonder,
And I have looked and found you beside me,
Your eyes directed toward the magnificence of our creator too.
And when you have contemplated… meditated… slept… or prayed,
Did you not hear the quiet rustle of my garment,
And feel me settle down beside you?
A thought beginning in my mind
Ends in yours.
Your presence, for me, is so soft
So quiet and so close,
As mine is for you,
Yet I never doubt that you are there.
God and I are, among many things, companion to you.
Peace is not nothingness,
And God and I can be as unobtrusive
As curtains blowing in a room.

Leave your consciousness,
Come into mine.
You will find that consciousness, too,
Is your own.
So many people want to take their ideas and beliefs,
Even their perceptions,
From the consciousness they are presently in
And bring these into higher consciousness
Or Christ Consciousness,
Believing that what they bring will take on
Deep new meaning or a fresh new glow.
People do not realize that, in Christ Consciousness,
These prized treasures may have no meaning.
They may have no place at all.
When you come into a consciousness
Higher than the one you have been in,
Put everything as you have known it down.
Leave everything behind.
Come with no expectation
Or desire to measure or compare.
Come to soak in and to enjoy.
Live moment by moment
In the higher consciousness.
Let it give to you all that it holds.
For when what you find here inspires you,
But no longer impresses you…

When you are no longer impressed with yourself
For being here,
Then you are no longer a visitor.
Then you are beginning to build yourself a home.

Sometimes you think you will take
The way you see into higher consciousness
And your perception will be made so much grander
Because you have done this.
But that is like taking your sunglasses
Or a pair of binoculars into Christ Consciousness.
To see the sun,
Your eyes are enough.

Forget what you have felt or seen.
Forget what you have believed to be true or false.
Isn't it free, standing here in higher consciousness?
What do you feel or see or believe now?
No one is telling you to be or not to be anything.
Whatever you get here,
You will get or get to be
By being in the moment,
And being free and innocent in the moment,
Open to anything.
Higher consciousness is just that.
Take a deep breath of higher consciousness.
Isn't it invigorating
Like fresh mountain air?
You can almost taste the freedom.
Take another deep breath and stay a while.
You suddenly realize you are not just human,
Or just anything.

I came to all of you to be a body,
But what I shared with you was not of the body.
It was of God's mind and heart…
Universal truth and love.
As I came to you,
Come to me,
Not as a body,
But as the eternal being you are.
Keep company with me,
As I kept company with you.
Let us demonstrate and share the truth,
Merely by being what we truly are.
Come be with me.
Come to a space inside your own mind and heart.
It is free there.
If you lay down everything you have known as a body,
You are free to be yourself.
Here, you will discover God has never been angry at you.
And we have always been friends.
You will feel power without threat or pain.
It is more a powerful sense or well-being
That makes you not want to hurt,
Or hurt anyone,
And causes you to realize
You have never been
Or will never be alone.

And Now God

I have felt your self-doubt,
And your doubt of me.
I have heard you say,
"I wonder if I can."
"I can not" or "I never will."
Hear me now and know that what I say is true.
For all time,
And for whatever you try to manifest,
And for whatever you aspire to be or do.
I provide… I provide.
Also what you think you need within your being
Is already there.
You have been provided with what you need
To manifest or become.
You have the power to access all the knowledge there is,
And the ability to draw to you anything that was created,
And the ability to create more.
What I created,
I created for me and you.
As for your dream of not being able to manifest,
I stand beside you,
Ready to assist.
I tell you,
I provide… I provide.

I who have no fear,
I who know and am the truth
And have no sense of hopelessness or shame,
I have shrunk down in my greatness,
To deliberately experience hunger
That I might also experience being fed by you.
And, as you did so,
It was not the food you gave that satisfied me,
But your beauty,
As you expressed your compassion and generosity.
It pleases me so much to experience you
Expressing and demonstrating what of me
I placed in you.
What I value,
You are.
Though I need no hands to reach you
I have become an open hand
To feel you extend your own hand
And fit it into the hand I opened before you.
You are so beautiful.
I am so moved by you.
I will become ill or weak,
Joyful or strong,
To interact with you
And to feel you interact with me,
What you really are…
And what you can become.
When you sit in the dark and cold.
Attending to what lays feeling helpless and afraid,
We exchange places, for awhile.

Then it is YOU keeping company with ME,
Sending energy,
Changing fear.
As you are with me in such a night,
I will be with you wherever you are in your life
Or in consciousness.
In all your days and nights,
I will be with you.
You are my beloved son,
I am well pleased.

It is okay,
You can wake up now.
You are here,
You are home,
You are safe,
You are loved.

BOOK 3

Listen

Hold very still and listen to me.
You are my favorite child,
My only one.
I love you.
So often you vibrate.
Ask me to touch you
So you can become still.
Then you can sense me,
Then you will know.

You steered yourself toward planet earth,
Like a sailor making a journey,
And I accompanied you.
You, like a seaman sailing his ship,
I, like the ship you sailed,
The wind… the sun… and the water.
We were never separate, during that brave journey.
We are not separate now.
You were not sure what to expect,
But you knew you must come.
I came, also, to experience this life with you
And to be your God… your companion… your love… and your friend.
You will know me all of these ways, during a lifetime.
I find the channels,
I create the ways.
And always I am your God.
Did you know you came to heal and be your own power?
You came, also, to be loved and to be love
And to demonstrate the relationship we have together.
You came to master a life (your life),
And to conquer a world (your world),
And then to stretch and enjoy what resulted from that.
You knew you could do it, before you came.
You knew you lacked the experience you sought,
But not what it took to have the experience.
You came where it would be harder,

To test and feel your power,
And to heal a planet that needed healing.
I needed you to come,
And you needed to come.
I am here still,
Just by your shoulder.

Be a wishing well,
Fill yourself with wishes.
Do not put any fear
Or mistrust into what you are wishing.
I will be the wishes and the well.
I will be the request and the answer.
Do not worry.
Consider to whom you are entrusting your wishes...
Me.
I know your wishes before you make them,
And I know they are already answered
Before you live them.
Discouragement delays the package coming.
It creates a vibration around you
That makes the gift hard to find you.
It as if you've called in an order,
Then rearranged your house numbers
So the mail carrier cannot find you.
I always know where you are.
Send me your wishes
And some trust.
I will make sure the answered wish finds you.
And if, in anger, you send it back
I will look in your heart.
If I see the longing for it still there,
I will send it again...
Maybe in a way you will not, at first, recognize it.
You cannot trick or think God into not being God,
No matter what you trick or think yourself into believing,
Because you are so set on believing

God does not answer and that you are a victim.
If you have asked, even once,
You will be answered.
Don't worry.
You are whom I love,
I cannot say no to you.

I created you
So we could be so many ways together.
The child-parent relationship
Is not the only relationship we can enjoy.
Any relationship you have on the earth plane
Can become a relationship you have with me.
The relationship you have with nature,
You can have with me.
The relationship you have with music,
You can have with me.
The relationship you have with your cat
You can have with me also.
Know this too:
In all your relationships,
You have a relationship with me.
I am so much more than parent,
I am so much more than child.
I am all things and in all things.
Be open to experiencing me,
As I am always experiencing you.

Men think I count the number of times
They attend a church service or mass.
They believe I am counting each kind act
And weighing it against each bad one.
I am interested in what each of you carries
In his heart and soul...
All that is there before it ever expresses as an act,
All that one does or dreams of doing.
And I know what created what I see there.
I see... I know, all the time.
There is not a second I am not seeing or not knowing.
I not only see and know you,
I experience you.
You are like a meat I eat,
A wine I drink.
You are the open flower I smell,
The song I sing,
The pattern of a thousand twinkling lights
I gaze at.
As I am the breeze on your face,
You are like unto a wind on mine.
I experience you,
And I am pleased... so very pleased
With that I see and experience and know.

The PAST is a cold burned out star,
Existing only in the mind.
You are mine,
Yet you have your freedom.
You have belonged to many lifetimes,
Many universes.
What starts out, in a lifetime,
As being all there is
Creates, in you, a desire to find more…
A dark and cold
That drives you to seek light and fire,
It serves you,
Then it is done.
You are in the beginning of a great learning
And transformation.
A hunger will be satisfied.
You think you hunger for love,
Your hunger for what you came here to do is greater.
It will be satisfied.

Over and over again,
You relive loneliness
And the sense of being unloved.
These are the feelings you experienced when you first came here for an
    incarnation.
It was a new sensation for you,
And it made you feel afraid…
It also made you forget
That we came together.
I tell you this:
I did not create you to be alone,
I did not ask you to come here to be alone,
And you did not agree to come
Where there would be none to love you.
No such place exists.
Actually, a part of my love for you
Exists in everything I created.
A part of my love for everything I created
Exists in you.
Fear and a false sense of being separate and alone,
Or being at war with other things created
Get in the way of accessing that love,
But it is alright.
This is not a permanent condition,
And always there exists for everything I created
The opportunity to be loved by everything else I created.
Did you know my other creations that do not look like you can
Very personally and very truly love you?
And, through them, I love you.
What happens is the love, placed in you by me,

Is recognized and felt.
It is a feeling of finding home,
And what has found you out leans toward you,
As a flower leans toward the sun
Or a cool refreshing breeze or water.
Everything created can feel this
For everything else created,
And it happens when the love I placed in my creations
Is discovered and felt.
It is a natural response,
A leaning of creations toward their creator.
Some animals and flowers hove actually loved you.
Some aliens and other entities from other places
Have and do love you.
Spirits and angels have and do love you.
The elements and elementals have loved you.
And, out of these moments of discovery and loving,
Some of my creations have formed a relationship with you
That has gone beyond the moment and will last forever.

I speak truth…
There is no reason to defend myself,
Or to convince you.
I say this to you and it is true,
Though you live the thoughts and feelings it is not.
Your truth and mine is this:
You did not come here to be alone.
You did not come alone,
I came with you.
I have created all things to love you
And be loved by you.
Some of these have loved you…
Do love you… will love you.
Take your time,
Be easy with yourself.
I will make sure
All that love you
Will find you.

Sometimes you are put together
With one who helps you remember me.
I am pleased,
For, in remembering me,
You are also remembering yourself.
I am always helping you remember
For, as you remember,
You become, once again, sure of our relationship…
The most important thing of all.
So many of you come,
Knowing you will forget me,
But sure you will find me again.
And so you make the journey,
For reasons that honor me
And strengthen and expand yourselves.
Fear teaches you that you were wrong or forced to come,
And that you and I do not have a relationship that endures.
Yet do you know why you were so sure, in the beginning,
That you would remember me?
Because I promised that, even should you forget me,
You would not be totally responsible for remembering me.
I promised you
I would help you remember,
And that is what I do.

You may not know this,
But, when you are angry,
And reciting fear-lessons taught to you,
You are calling me.
I hear you in silence and in noise.
You think you have to be angry
And putting on a noisy show,
To get my attention…
To make me know how much you want me,
How much you want "us".
You want there to be "us" not just "you".
I hear you and love you,
Through silence and through noise.
I will always help you.
I say there is not just "you",
There is always "us",
Because it is the truth.
But I know you believe you are alone,
And that we have not been well acquainted
And loving each other since the beginning,
Before time.
Even before I created you,
I loved you.
You moved in me.
I felt you and knew you as part of myself
I must express outwardly.
I began to create what lived in me,
Only, now, I could experience it also outside.
There has never been just "you".
There has always been "us".

But I know you feel it is not so.
You feel alone.
I can help you better when you do not vibrate
With fear's teaching.
I love you.
I hear you in silence d in noise.
And I will always help you.
And I will always be with you.

Do not think life is just for healing.
From the first trauma (birth),
And the traumas that followed that,
We have been doing much together,
And have much more to do…
We have much to do and enjoy.
As you come into your own power,
Which you are doing now,
You will begin to sense life
Is more an adventure.
For that is what life is.
That is what your life is,
An adventure we are having together.

You are used to dressing yourself in certain emotions...
Assigned to you or borrowed from the first ones
Around you,
The ones you call family.
Why do you, so often, wear such dark garments,
When you are made of light,
And you have wings?

In the relationship of husband and wife,
You and I
Find yet another way
To love each other.

Channeled from Quan Yin

(The female part of God expressing)

The path connecting you to me
Is like a ribbon of silk.
It runs throughout eternity.
Make light of fear.
It is poor and feeble...
A midget imitating a giant,
And it babbles.
I focus on truth,
I accept only truth,
And I call upon you
To call upon truth and God and me.
The path exists forever.
It begins in heaven,
Winds throughout lifetimes,
And goes on into eternity.
In your heart and in your mind,
Come home to God and me.
Rest with us awhile,
Or laugh with us,
Or let us hold you.
We have had such good times,
You and I.
You are beloved.
I seek constantly the channels
To use to reach you.
Your mind is the best channel of all.
That is why fear tries to occupy your thoughts so often,
So you are tied up with it,
Rather than riding your consciousness home with me.

Yet it can never divide us.
Music, color, loving hearts, your dreams…
Through them, I touch you.
Yet, in consciousness, you can come
Directly to me.
As soon as you wish it,
We are together.
See me at my temple.
Sit with me and let me hold your head
And serve you tea.
We can talk of anything…
Our conversations can be light or important.
Or there can be beautiful silences.
We are not lost to each other.
That is impossible.
I wish to put pictures in your head
That replace the pictures fear has put there.
Imagination can be a tool for truth.
Play with pretty thoughts and imaginings.
You will be surprised what truth they bring you.

A Message from Christ

I see you... I always see you.
I see, also, what you live with...
That which is in your outer world
And what is in your mind.
I am your brother
And your guide through the human experience you are having.
I keep my divinity,
Yet know what it is like to be human.
I have forgotten neither humanness nor divinity.
Both hold a sacred place in my consciousness.
I am quiet in my guidance,
But that does not mean I am weak or disinterested.
My concern for you is real,
And my message mighty.
I do not give up or falter.
I stay to guide you and to help you.
I still teach the same truth...
The only truth...
That you and God are one.
That you are not separate from God or the kingdom of heaven.
I still send the same message from my father...
And that is come to God,
And be fulfilled and expanded and healed of forgetfulness,
By that relationship.
I am here for you forever,
Your loving guide and brother.
Often, as when you were young,
I stay in your room,
When you sleep at night.

From the Holy Messengers:

Do not stay silent,
Talk to us AND listen.
Write to us,
Let us write through you.

I am God,
Everything is me expressing.
I experience all that I created.
All that I created,
While having an individual experience,
Is also experiencing me.
I am not afraid of myself.
I ask that you not be afraid of yourself,
And that, in the end, you always turn to me for truth.
Your smaller consciousness has often tricked you
Into holding onto a lie.
But I cannot lie to you.
Come to me when you want the truth.
My truth (THE ONLY TRUTH), will inform you
Or transform you,
But it will not hurt you.
The greatest and the smallest is dear to me.
In knowing the truth,
You will also know that you are safe.

You love me.
When you war against me,
You war against yourself
And the natural love you hold for me.
It is like being pulled apart
By your own hands.
"Punishment... Payback... Retribution"
What are these?
A fearful consciousness invented them,
They do not issue from me.
What misunderstandings these concepts bring.
The truth is
WE love each other.

God Speaks in Plural

As the sun follows the moon.
We watch you.
We know, at times, you are afraid.
As we ask you to have faith in us,
We have faith in you.
You are all things to us,
As we ask you to believe
We are all things.
Everything we have asked you to believe of us,
Through prophets… and channels…
And personal insights and dreams,
We believe of you.
The relationship you are asked, in love, to have with us
We already have with you.
We ask you to love us and trust us.
As much and more, we love and trust you.
We ask you to relax and communicate with us
And interact with us.
We are always communicating and interacting with you.
We believe in what we created.
We believe in you.
To come home to us,
Is to come home to all the belief
And love and trust we have for you.
We see you as you truly are.
We know your highest purpose,
And that you are truly committed to it…
So committed that you will fulfill it,
However long it takes.
We always have you.

We always experience you.
When we ask you to come home to us,
Through prayer or meditation,
Or whatever means serves you,
In whatever moment serves you,
We ask you to do this so you will know
What we already know:
Our relationship,
You… who you truly are and what you are truly all about,
Our love… and the love you are… and the love you have for us,
Our faith in you and the faith you have in us.
Come home often, beautiful one…
Relax and come home,
You have never really left it.
Use any relaxed moment (doing anything or doing nothing),
Rather than a long exercise,
When that serves you best.
A moment home brings everything into balance…
The spirit and all of the cells in your body are glad.
Any moment you say Father… Mother… God,
And open,
You will know we are here.
We are always here.

When you step back from creating and look around,
You want to go back and create again.
There is a feeling of joy to do this.
When you step away from fear and doubt and flawed perception,
You want to go back to love and be loved.
There is a feeling of joy and courage to do this.
Then you are thinking and feeling clearly.
Then you are not merely thinking like God,
Because you are in the same clear consciousness,
You ARE God thinking
And so you come back to do it again,
With all the joy and courage and intention
To do it as God would do it.
You are God coming to live a life on the physical plane.
If you get caught up again in the consciousness
That teaches fear and doubt,
And brings forgetfulness
(Not only of God, but of yourself... your God Self),
You still are that God Self,
Ready and able to create
And ready and able to love and be loved.
That Self, in the deepest part of you,
Has not forgotten.
It remembers and is your reminder.
All of your lifetimes it will work to remind you,
And to express and do what it willingly...
Lovingly... joyously... courageously came here to do.
You are your own hope and celebration.

That is why fear would teach you that you are worthless,
And that all is hopeless.
It is trying to upstage you,
Steal your show and become the star.
You are the star... the creator... the lover...
The God that came to live a life on the physical plane.
Your God Self knows you can do it,
And that you will do it.
One time, you will do it all
And, then, you will not return.
Not because you have served a sentence that is over,
But because you will have completed a life
That is as perfect as you planned it,
Before you began it.
You and God will embrace,
And weep for the joy,
The beauty,
And the triumph
Of what you have done.
You will have fulfilled a perfect dream or yours
And God's,
And only you could have done it.
You and God knew that,
Before you began.
And nothing created or dreamed,
Along the way to fulfilling that dream,
Will be as beautiful.
It will be the happy ending to living life,
On the physical plane.
In this, no one finishes last.
No one fails.

This is perfect creation,
Not a competition.
And, after the perfect creation…
On to other glories.
God and you are never done.

BOOK 4

You

You are a part of God
It could not keep to itself,
But had to share.
You are what is loved by God.
God is in love with what it created.
God is in love with You.
Ask a man, "What is love?"
That man might say, "God is love."
Ask God, "What is love?"
God will say, "Love is You."

You are what is inside your heart,
After all the fear and darkness,
Like cobwebs,
Are cleared away.
You are what is inside your heart –
What is placed there by God.
What is really there.
What never leaves,
But what expresses and creates and recreates itself
Over and over again.
If you could look inside your heart,
As though you were looking through a window,
You would see light,
And limitless energy and creativity…
And many other lovely things.
You would see unlimited potential
And possibility,
For that is how you were created.
And if you looked inside the heart of God,
You would see yourself.
It sounds too good to be true.
But it is true.

While your creator is knowable,
Your creator is also beyond all knowledge.
It cannot be contained in a single philosophy,
Belief system, or thought.
You are of that greatness and unlimitedness.
What you are cannot be contained in a single lifetime.
What you are exists, at the same time, on different levels
In other places, and in other times.
You cannot know or explain yourself or your creator
Merely by what you are experiencing in your present earth lifetime.
There is a part of you, right now, existing on a spiritual realm
That grows more divine and beautiful by what you are doing in this life
And in other lives in other places.
When you say, about your earth home,
"I would like to leave this place."
That other part of you says "No,"
Because of where you are in that other shining place.
Your stopping your experience here
Would certainly affect the experience you are having there.
The True Self (the self that knows) says "No,"
And so you grow and unfold and, even here,
Become more than what you were.
And still, you have the ability to change and create and re-create.
You are creative.
The source of yourself is vast, limitless, great.
You cannot be explained by a single lifetime or many lifetimes.
What you are is more than the lives you live,
Or how you live them.
You, as love, go on and on
Affecting and changing and being changed.

You are the force and energy of your lifetimes,
And what goes on before them and after them.
What does God's love look like?
It looks like you.

You see yourself as something small
Endeavoring to know something big.
You are limitless,
As is your God.
There is more of you to know
Than you shall ever know in a lifetime,
Or many lifetimes.
Yet, do not make it a race to know.
Just be – and, every moment, get a sense of yourself.
When you are with us… one of us…
As you are over and over again,
You know.
And even though part of knowing is being aware,
There will always be more to know –
When you are here, there is not the hunger and the fear
To have all the knowledge,
As there is when you are living a lifetime.
Yogananda was a master – on the Earth plane,
He is a growing master and a student here.
You are delighted there is more to learn,
When God is your favorite subject.
…You ponder your lifetimes…
You take them very seriously.
Yet you do not give a lot of thought to the times you were here,
During and between those lifetimes,
And that time you were here before the journey of lifetimes ever began.

By God's love…
You individualized,
As your journey began.
So many dreams,
So many beginnings and endings –
Only to begin and end, and begin again.
You have influenced all that is.
You have been what you despised
And what you loved.
Yet your true nature develops,
Grows more beautiful and blesses as it continues.
You are a vibration that is heard,
Throughout the universe.
You are an energy enjoyed by God.
Simply by being, you have changed universes
And been changed by this world,
And other worlds,
And, what dwells on them and in them.
You cannot know all that you are,
And how you influence and what you influence,
And what influences you.
Your essence and your thoughts travel
And are shared by brothers inhabiting other universes.
All this goes on and the spirit knows
And is not afraid.
Fear would tell you the Divine Self is callous
Because it does not save you from experiences.
It is not callous,
It is simply not afraid.
It is a caring Self that knows,

And so it says, "Yes… let's go on."
Take a deep breath.
Get a sense of what it knows…
Of what you know,
And then go on.

The roles you play,
Like robes worn then cast off,
Will bring you much.
Is it so important that many times you were a ruler –
Hated by people, in some lifetimes,
Dearly loved in others?
Is it so important that you were a cobbler,
A lawyer,
A merchant,
A loner,
A family man,
Lover to a soul mate,
Spouse to many others,
In marriages both good and bad?
Is it so important?
What is important is this:
By living lifetimes,
You will go from valuing power,
To valuing God.
You will learn how to have the human experience
And never leave the spirit out;
That, while being human,
You will demonstrate and look to God.
And, although the world does not always feel comfortable,
You will not be at odds with heaven,
But at home.

"A Message from the Divine Ones"

What are you like?
You are like us.
What are you?
You are us.
When you are in a consciousness
That sees yourself as separate… different from us,
You will disagree.
But what we say is the truth.
We look at you,
We see ourselves,
An individualized expression of the Divine One.
We are aware of this about ourselves and you,
You are not.
By the way,
You have sat in bliss too.
There is no shame or selfishness in this.
You have sat in bliss too
And watched the dreams unfold.
Like us, you have sat and watched –
Not to smirk or be entertained,
But to understand…
To learn in order to know and assist.
Being in bliss is the best way to do this.
Because, in the state of bliss, fear is absent.
Brother… comrade… friend,
Fellow individualized expression of the Divine One,

Yet, at the same time,
Always a part of the whole,
You move inside of God,
And you have always been there with us.

You are us.
You are part of God eternal,
Individualized and expressing.
What we do here,
You do here also.
When you purposely shrink yourself
And filter down to have a lifetime,
Part of you stays here,
And part of you begins a journey
That will bring you something you have wanted to learn or master.
You also give to a world that becomes more
Because you are in it.
You get a chance to practice and enhance
Your God-like qualities and abilities.
But, through it all, you are still you
And you are still us.
When you are not mankind,
You observe mankind
And send guidance.
What you attempt to do on earth,
You do in a greater way in heaven.
Guidance is geared mainly to wake a person up,
So he will get on being God in his human experience,
And not become just more and more human.
You are asked to trust that you—
And that you and God—are more than you know.
You can never know everything in your human experience,

So you are asked to trust, so more understanding and awareness will
come.
Trust allows you to BE,
And BEING brings you the awareness the world will never teach you.

"Change"

You are courageous when it comes to change.
You have used change… transformation
In many lifetimes as your tool for progress.
What you are really endeavoring to change…
What you have always been endeavoring to change,
Is the experience you are having of yourself.
You want to feel yourself another way.
You endeavor to change the experience you are having of yourself.
You want others to share that changed experience of you,
Once you have achieved it.
You have never NEEDED to change.
You were never created to change
Because something was wrong with you.
You were created to grow… expand…
Experience your changed self
And know variety.
You have an innate ability to do this.
The clogged chakras,
The dull and darkened mind,
The heaviness of body and soul
Can make you misinterpret and mistrust yourself.
You are a physical being.
You are a being of light.
You can flood your chakras with light,
Or leave them clogged with residue of a thousand years.
You can change cells,
You can change your mind.

There are changes because the body and soul are willing.
What you are was created to experience itself in different ways,
And expand, doing this.
What you are, survives and surpasses the madness of this world.

Enlightenment is knowing you are divine,
Not human,
And neither is your God.
You are both divine.
And you are having a divine relationship with your God.
How could you have any other?
You are constantly creating and re-creating yourself,
That is one thing you do when you live a lifetime.
God creates and re-creates itself, through you.
If you were not on earth, having a lifetime,
And if you were not on the spirit plane,
During and between lifetimes,
You would be someplace else having a lifetime
Creating and re-creating yourself and God.
For you are very creative,
And eager to know what else there is.
You are pursuing knowledge and creating knowledge,
At the same time.
Some people claim to have lived only one lifetime.
Don't believe it or be impressed.
If what they say were true,
They would be both unproductive
And uncreative, at the same time.
They would be limited as a contributor.
Christ has stayed very involved with your earth plane.
He still works there,
And is felt there.

He might as well be having a lifetime there.
He did not ascend to sneak off and play it safe and comfortable.
He understands how he and his creator work together,
And is pleased when there is something for them to do.

BOOK 5

Rest Comfortably in Me

You are energy,
You are light,
You are the power
And love of God expressing
And whatever else
You want to be.
You have choice.
Pick something... anything,
And be it!

You are me.
Don't you understand?
You are part of me expressing.
I am the greatest of you
(All that you could ever be—
You taken to the highest and more.)
We can be mirrors for each other.
Like me, you are many things at once.
Unlike me, you are not aware of all you are and all you can be.
Also, you are unaware that you are all at once.
You think you are someone or something.
But that is just where you put your focus.

I rest comfortably in you.
I willingly and joyfully channel through you
And look from out your eyes.
I move in you and through you.
You are more than this –
(A temple, a space for me.)
Certainly you are more,
But for the sake of the point I wish to make,
You are bed and temple and a home for me.
I am comfortable in you,
I am not lessened or defiled,
Resting in you.
You are not dark or evil.
There is no reason to be afraid.

Be comfortable in knowing
That the qualities you look for in God,
You already have.
What you want God to be,
You are.
God, being the source,
Is all powerful and complete
In what it is,
But you are of the source
And possess all of its qualities, characteristics and abilities and possibilities,
As you discover God – you discover yourself.
If you have not discovered or used or perfected What you are,
It is because you have not given thought to it.
You will not entertain the idea that you could be so vast...
So loving...
So powerful.
This is too much for your
Worldly identity to bear.
Even the possibility of being so much
Feels heavy
And implies too much responsibility.
What, if being so much, you should fail
At what is expected of you – by others and by God and yourself?
What a sin that would be.
It would be like losing God all over again,
And so the dread of being divine builds.
It begins to feel like something you don't want.
And so you tell yourself,
It cannot be – your worldly self is afraid.
It has been abused by power and, at other times, by power been the abuser.

Yet the power that you and God are is not the power – as the world
would know it.
The power of you and God is creative, loving (without fear),
And free.
It feels like freedom, and has within it the desire to create and to love.
This is you as power.
What you think you are is afraid; therefore,
You consider power to be Force.
When you have thoughts about Who you are – consider
There are two of you.
There is you afraid, and there is you not afraid.
When you are without fear, you are vast, energetic and eager to be and
be more.
Then you are truly Who you are; and, then, you are like God.

Close your eyes,
Take a deep breath…
Connect with me
To know what you are to me –
To know how I experience you,
And I am always experiencing you.
You are music
That plays to me
And in me
All day and all night long.
My heart is full of you.
I am in love with you.
I am enriched and inspired by you.
I am extended by you.
I do not feel endangered by you.
I am not discouraged by you.
You cannot lose my interest or my love.
I see the mistakes you have made
And the abomination you have committed by your fears and the
    thought forms
This fear has created.
I am appalled by these abominations.
I am not appalled by you,
For nothing I have created is ever lost to me altogether.
In fact, a part of everything created
Has remained with me
Since the beginning.
The part of you that left,
Left to experience me
And extend me.

That part, over and over again,
Has been sidetracked by fear.
But I, who am without fear,
Continue with you and know you
For the clean, beautiful, unspoiled creation
Of God that you are.
I tell you
You are my music,
And I say
Play on and on.

In me,
Rest as comfortably
As I rest in you.
Rest knowing I have never abandoned you,
And that I never will.
I cannot.
You are me.
As I am you.
I am the creator
And cannot be uncreated.
Neither can you.
It is impossible,
And we cannot be separated.
We have a relationship,
And you think of it as an earthly relationship
Which can be severed,
And is based on rewards… punishments…
Deserving… competition, ETC.
That is not our relationship.
There is no human understanding of it.
In trying to impart an understanding,

Consider the earth, with all life and water upon it,
And the moon and stars above it –
All seeming to exist separately,
Yet all existing together.
Even this does not really describe it,
Yet it is closer to the truth
Than thinking of two people who might
Leave each other at any time,

And who might change their minds about each other
Because of judgment.
Judgment does not exist in our relationship,
Judgment was created by the ego.
Our relationship is the you and me – THE ONE,
Existing with the elements of creative energy
And individual expression.
As you create and change, I do too,
Yet I am constant in my place of power (love eternal).
You are changeable yet constant in your place of power (my love for
    you eternal).
My love for you never stops.
It is impossible for me not to love you.
It is impossible for me not to love.
You are made of me and from me… love…
Love that does not end.
Another way of looking at us is this;
Consider us a single breath, or, at least, the process of breathing.
You cannot take apart the process of breathing and eliminate anything.
If you did, there would be no breathing. We are one breath,
Making all life possible.
To know your strength, understand my strength.
To know your love, understand my love.
To know you, understand me –
Not as an entity separate from you, but as pure energy…
Pure light… pure strength…
Pure love always with you
And a part of you
(A part of you, not apart from you.)

Strive to be conscious of ME and YOU AND ME,
As I am of us and you.
You know how you are feeling when you are not feeling judgment.

You are able to appreciate what is.
You would say you are having a good day.
Judgment does not exist for me,
So I am always having a good day,
And I am always able to appreciate you.

Do not think of yourself as an entity.
Think of yourself as pure consciousness, pure love, and pure energy.
Believe that you expand and flow.
Feel yourself as a force too powerful not to make a difference.
See yourself as Light.
See yourself as Color.
Know that you are softness.
Believe you are these and more,
At the same time.
Your awareness is a spot light
You put on yourself (a part of yourself or all of yourself),
Yet there is always something more that you are
That you haven't discovered, developed,
Or lived yet.

I created you and gave you the ability to go on creating yourself.
Therefore, you are divine potential,
Able to develop and become more at any time.

⊹⟞⊜⟝⊹

I have known you forever,
And I have experienced you
Calling yourself by many different names
And in conflict with many different identities.
I have always known this too:
That you will survive everything
And go on to be you –
A divine creation,
Beloved by what created you.
I have not been indifferent,
But neither have I interfered;
For I made you a creator
And you must be allowed to be that.
Even your faulty creation
Will help mold you to be

The divine creator
I know you to be.
By your creations will you know me.
Faulty creations
Bring false knowledge
But, by recognizing the false,
Tearing it down,
And rebuilding again,
You come to know – not only
The wonder and greatness of me,
But also the wonder and greatness of you.
Like me, you create

And become part of your creation.
You are both story and storyteller,
Music and musician,
Artist and the picture painted…
Like me,
You are every part of the creation.
You are paint, and words
Notes and color…
You are the force and the energy –
The vibration and the sound,
The inspiration
And visualization
That goes into
Creating,
And the thing created.

You are creator,
Creation, and the creative process –
What is behind it
And within.
If you were free of judgment and fear,
Your creations would be without judgment and fear,
And you would enjoy creating.
You would realize that, like me,
You are in love with creating;
And you are in love with what is created.
Also – fear tells you to stop –
But truth wants you to create more from it.
You can create a life, a world.
You can go on creating forever.
And creator: remember this –

In your creating,
Do not forget to include me.
I am your prime ingredient,
Your most important component,
And your co-creator.

You were and are
My inspiration,
And should be your own.
I do not ask that you
Look to me for inspiration,
But that you look to yourself –
For you are everything divine and good,
Holy and whole.
And if you do look for me –
Even then,
Look to yourself

For I am there
In you,
Not separate in you,
But a part of you.
I am your Center
You are my heart.
We are never apart,
We are One,
We are whole.
We are a single breath,
And, as we breathe,
Creation begins and continues.

Enlightenment is remembering.
What you get, in reaching it,
Is what you didn't already know.
Enlightenment is a point of awareness –
It is inevitable.
Think of it as an airport
Or a train station –
A place of arriving

Where, eventually, everybody comes:
Some by bus or train,
Some by plane,
Some on foot,
Some flying.
Enlightenment:
Everyone will create
His own experience of it,
And it is a moment by moment
Present moment experience.
God and your ego –
Both speak in the present moment,
But you will only hear the one
That you give your attention to.
For years,
You listened to your ego.
More than you did, this year.
There was a time when
You mistook the ego's voice
For God's –
No more!

Believe you have gained and grown
And benefited because of this.
When at an early age, you said, "I will know God -"
That was your spirit expressing.
When you said it had to be by a certain year,
That was your Ego talking.
When your Ego talks…
Stop listening.

Kuan Yin:
Goddess of Kindness and Mercy

(The part of God that stayed behind)

Your slippered foot
Was on the silver stair.
You could have started up
But, for the time it took to care,
You looked back
And decided not to climb.
You surrendered heaven
And stayed behind
To offer balm and silence
To a wounded and unquiet world.
Kuan Yin –
My gold amythest – pink Goddess,
My light,
My friend.
Thank you for being
Where last hope ends,
To take my hand,
When, into that dark deep abyss,
I fall,
And teach me, by your kind gentleness,
To understand
That God and I do love each other, after all.

⋅→⇒◦⇐←⋅

Note to the reader: I was given the last line by spirit and told to write
    a poem by myself, but the last line, given by spirit, would have to
    be the ending to the poem.

~ 142 ~

Message from Kuan Yin

What a long time it has been my friend,
Since we sat and drank tea in my temple on the hill.
There was you and the music of moving branches then –
Not a bird or a cricket was still.
I served you hope and you gave me joy.
I was your Goddess and you were my dear mortal boy.
How sophisticated God has become in your mind,
As you explore different faiths and philosophies.
And how far you have traveled from me!
Do you know that God does not crave your respect,
But yearns for your intimacy?
I long for you too –
Come back to the temple and rest and take tea.
Let God sing through the birds,
And shake the fragrant blossoms of the trees.
We have words and thoughts to exchange,
And dreams to fulfill.
The simple path is unchanged,
We wait on the hill.

◇━◉ ◉━◇

Note to the reader: I wrote this poem but was told to use it in David's book. Creative writing is not channeled writing but I do believe we do nothing alone. Even in creative writing, spirit still creates with us.

Kuan Yin's Reply to a Prayer for Love

I have made your back strong
Against the wind's relentless push and power.
On that same wind,
I have sent you the sound of laughter,
The song of birds,
The sweetest scent of flowers.
You asked me for a loved one
To share your heart and home,
Because you are alone.
He has not come yet,
So you sit and fret.
It does not mean he will not come.
It does not mean, when he is near,
I will not send to him a dream,
And put in it a path to you
For him to follow.
He will find you.
Until that time,
Keep this in mind:
When there are many…
When there are few…
When there are none,
There is God and there is me,
And the kind sun above you,
And the cruel wind behind you.

Kuan's Plea for Return

In the great heart of God,
There is a longing for the return
Of all that it created.
Yet, it would not have you be
Where you would not stay.
You are free.
It is love's way.
You did not know you could break
The heart of God,
Did you?
You did not know you are missed,
As you have missed absent family members,
Absent lovers,
An absent friend.
In your own heart there is a longing too.
Come back to be with God again.

BOOK 6

Love and the Wrong Classroom

Love and going home –
The gentler you make
The journey,
The farther you will go.

Love is,
It simply is,
And it is enough.

1.

For lifetimes, you have been in the wrong classroom listening to the wrong teacher. Your ego has been talking to you about love for a long time now, and using the products of ego teaching as demonstrations of its accuracy. Your spirit is your rightful teacher. It's knowledge is universal truth and it takes its instruction from God. You will be surprised how different the lessons are and how different the experiences are when you switch to the right classroom with the only correct instructor. Anything that you question or do not understand… anything that bothers you, you can take to spirit and get the truth.

2.

Let us put you in the right classroom, right now. As you read the following pages, even if what they are saying does not sound correct, please accept that they are. It is what your ego has been telling you about God, yourself, and love, that makes you skeptical. You have had years

of negative, hopeless conditioning. Now, block out the ego's objections
and listen to the truth.

3.

The flower turning to the sun is love.
The child opening its arms to be lifted is love.
Your whole being moving to music playing is love.
Your own thoughts stopping long enough to hear what another is saying —
     or stopping
long enough to hear the thoughts of God — is love.
Even reluctantly getting out of bed and getting dressed is love.
You are love set in motion,
By your God.
And you, in turn, set love in motion as you live your life.
Do not say you did not witness, demonstrate, or interact with love today.

4.

Love is me.
You are looking for me
And missing me
In all the places and in all the forms you go to, looking for love.
Instinctively, you sense that
What you think you must seek
Is very vast and very great.
Yet your thinking confines it to only certain forms: saying "I will find it in
     a woman or a man. It is there in a family, in beautiful things, in
     a favorite pet."
And so your losses exceed your gains.
It is everywhere for you

And in you, because I am in all things and in you –
To be enjoyed in form or formlessness.
I am in the universal thought tapes that play in your consciousness,
Turn off the worldly tapes and listen to me for a while.
I am in your heart, whether you are being moved by something outside
　　yourself or not.
Come be with me.
I keep you company within and without.
You have a relationship with love that has never ended.
I am ready to be with you in anything, at any time –
In whatever pleases you and what does not.
For I am always pleased with you.
It is you who are selective,
Choosing me in some things
And not in others,
Believing I am only in what pleases you
And only in what pleases you greatly.
Be selective, but do not let your selectivity convince you that you are limited
Or without or that I am limited. I am everywhere and I am everywhere
　　for you.
Did I ever think to be in a place or in a form where you could not find me?
NO! NO! NO!
What pleases you
Triggers your awareness,
Then you know.
When not being pleased, you are convinced I would choose to be with-
　　out you.
I guide you to the connections
That make sense and alleviate the madness.
Yet, in timelessness, we exist
Together
To move and be moved
By one another

And moved by the truth
That we ARE together –
Love and love
Forever and unending.

5.

God and your own soul – the part of God that is you –is the greatest
love in your life.
Interactions with anything else is for learning that.
There is some truth in the idea that God does not put as high a value
on romantic relationships as you do. God does not see the roman-
tic relationship as all – important, though you do.
That is because God knows the truth.
If you allow yourself to be guided by God, you will not miss these
relationships,
Nor will you be discouraged from having them.
But you will always be guided, in or outside these romantic relationships,
To have and enjoy the one true relationship there is – the relationship
you have with your own soul and God.
When you feel that relationship in all the relationships you can have in
the world, you will feel satisfaction and you will never be lonely.
You are not always in a relationship, by the world's standards.
And many people who are in a relationship still are not in a relation-
ship guided by love.
You are always in a relationship with your own soul and God.
And despite the emotions you are expressing or the untruths and half-
truths you are believing, at any time, that relationship is always
one of love.

6.

What is in front of you and moves your heart is your love in the moment,
And it does not have to be a person.
It is your most important love because it is the one to cause you to
    interact with your own heart.
Your love in the moment has nothing to do with past or future love.
It does not replace what else you are wanting to manifest. It is love
    NOW.
Connect with it.
What is love reminds you
That you are love.
That is what love in the moment does.

7.

God and your own soul resonate with the sameness of self.
It is harmony.
That is why what your soul wants, God wants too.
When you manifest and it falls short of what your soul has wanted,
There has been ego interference. You also experience lack of satisfaction
When you manifest what your ego not what your soul wants.
What God manifests, teaches God more about itself.
What comes through the manifestation empowers and enlightens.
It does not belittle or destroy.
If you listen and look for the truth, even your ill-favored manifestation
    will tell you
What assists to heal or empower.
If nothing else, it will show you what to add or eliminate in your man-
    ifestation process.

It will give you a chance to add, subtract, or make changes.
But a "bad manifestation" will never tell you about your ability to manifest.
The ego says it does, but it does not.
If you were sculpting with one hand bandaged and one hand free,
Could the bandaged hand really tell you what you could do with both
hands free?
And, regardless of whether you continue creating with truth or with some
Truth and the ego's lies, you keep creating.
It is what you and God do.
But do know that what you want from your soul, God wants too.
Your soul is God saying to itself, "I desire." God will note refuse itself.
It has no reason.

8.

When God became lonely, it created from itself what seemed outside
of itself
So it could interact with that and become satisfied.
You have that ability and it is what you do when you manifest.
You are actually manifesting all the time.
God can manifest without any fear or interference.
As you clear yourself, you manifest more and more clearly what your
soul wants.
But, at all times, you can call the greater power (God) into your
manifestation
To make it a clearer one.
You slow down your manifestation by judging or condemning it,
Yourself, or a greater power.
Your ego is afraid of more disappointment because it has judged itself a
Failure that will be destroyed by more failure.
It prefers that you stop trying to manifest.

It will not give you information you can use to continue with your
    manifestation –
Or to change it.
Nothing from God will ever tell you to stop manifesting, only your ego
    will do that.
Yet your ego's voice is futile.
You will never stop manifesting.

9.

When you relax, you are able to love in the present moment.
That is why it is important to relax when you are encountering some-
    one for
The first time.
Staying in the present moment, during an interaction, also enables you
    to get
The truth of the situation. You are able to get what it is telling you.
You are less apt to be distracted by what you think you should be getting.
You will be less apt to judge yourself, the other person, or the interaction.
Staying in the present moment, and not judging, doesn't make you kind –
You are already.
It makes you better informed.

10.

Spirit does not look favorably on what the world calls "dating."
Spending time lovingly with another
Is what the soul is craving when you find yourself reaching for another.
The soul wants, at the same time, its own company
And the company of another.
Dating, unfortunately, is often done out of loneliness,

Fear of being alone, pressure, and /or sexual excitement.
Based on this, the person dating has difficulty
Staying in the present moment.
Judgment arises, directed toward himself and the person he is with,
And he spends most of the time wishing he could feel a certain way
And reflecting on the past and future.
The gold of the present moment is lost and
One is left with many false assumptions.
Dating is not wrong or dangerous and not to be discouraged,
But it, in itself, is not what the soul is craving.
When there exists softness, enthusiasm, or simple curiosity
For what you are picking up about the other person –
Plus some degree of self-identification –
Dating can become a way of setting up a connection with that other person
To spend loving time with.
When spending time with someone, because of how you feel about the
    other person
And how you feel about yourself while being with that person
Is enough… then, dating is a good means for connecting, or further
    connecting.
When being with someone is about how you want to feel or what you
    want to get,
Dating serves no good purpose.
In fact, dating for these reasons can stimulate and increase what you
    are trying to escape,
Such as loneliness – or a feeling of being unlovable.
Dating is also not about falling in love –
Though certainly, over a period of dating for the right reasons, this can
    happen.
Dating should be about spending loving time with another.
It is about you enjoying the loving company of another,
While also feeling the loving company of your own soul.

11.

Loneliness is a feeling. Love is a fact.
When you are lonely, you think there is a lack of love.
Love always is and always is available.
This is not meant to void your feelings. Just understand,
If you have an issue with loneliness,
You do not have an issue with lack of love.
Lack of love is what loneliness feels like.
When you are lonely, you may also be missing what you want to manifest.
What is around you, but not in the present moment with you,
Has not come together with you yet.
It will.
When you are lonely, release the idea that you are without love.
Call upon your power of awareness, to enable you to feel love around you.
Acknowledge what you desire to manifest and send it your love.
Give it to God, at the moment of missing it.
Then open to the love, without and within you, for healing and
    confirmation
That you are with love;
You are not alone
Or without,
Only lonely.

12.

God does not know how to be and can never be FINISHED or NOT
    ENOUGH.
So why do you think love can be finished or not enough?
You are thinking YOU are finished or not enough.
Stop thinking it. Admit you do not know.
Creator, go back to your workbench. Look at what you want again.

Bring in your higher self and God.
God is perfect understanding. God, at any time, could do all the work.
But God created you as a "creator."
Yet, so many of you are creators who do not like their work.
But, instead of replacing your tools and rethinking or keeping the Vision,
You lay down your greatest tool (which is God)
And condemn the vision waiting to become a reality, behind your eyes.
Instead of saying of the work before you, "This displease me… it does
    not satisfy…
It is awful," you say it of yourselves.
Also quit calling what displeases you a mistake or testimony
To your inability to manifest.
You don't like it, but it is a manifestation
And it can tell you something if you let it.
It is like a bland stew that says, "I need salt," or
An over-seasoned stew that says, "I don't need so much embellishment."
Even an unsatisfying manifestation will not tell you that what you
    want you cannot have,
Or that you are not a manifester.
When you hear that, it is your ego talking.

13.

Another name for God is love.
Another name for you is love.
Nothing is without it –
For love is what made everything
And made everything of itself.
Love channeled itself and continues to channel itself
Through what it created.
There is no limited supply.
There is no luck or deserving or undeserving connected with it.

That is ego thinking.
To experience love is to access love already there,
For it is always present.
Accessing love is about awareness and acceptance.
It is not about supply or deserving.
It is hard for you to believe this,
But it is true.
Most people determine whether or not they possess love in themself,
Or in their life,
By whether or not they are in a relationship
And how that relationship is going.
If you are having difficulty manifesting a loving relationship,
Or are having a relationship that is unloving,
It is because of what you are thinking about yourself and relationships –
And what relationships represent to you.
It means you are doing a lot of ego listening.
Your experience with relationships has nothing to do with availability
Or supply of love,
Or your worthiness or unworthiness.
It is about your temporary inability to love yourself
Or see yourself as love.
It is not about your natural ability to love, and be love, and to draw
    like-love to you.
It is about What you are thinking and believing,
Because of What your ego is telling you.
Your ego will always discourage you about love
Because it feels unworthy of it and disconnected from it.
Your ego has a problem with God,
So it has a problem with love.
On your planet,
There is an obsession with ego thinking
And an acceptance of ego thinking as truth.
Whatever the ego says that you are,

You are not!
Whatever the ego tells you,
Is not the truth.
Listening to ego thinking is always discouraging.
Listening to the truth, on the other hand, is like
Listening to music play… As you listen,
You cannot help but feel larger and more free.
If you keep listening,
It unfolds wonderful revelations and insights.
It gives good news.
When you find it hard to listen to the truth,
Be aware of this: Love is.
It does not go away,
Or come to only certain ones.
It is not in one and not in another.

LOVE IS,
IT SIMPLY IS.
AND IT IS ENOUGH.

14.

There was to be the joy of love,
Not the hunger for it!
Desire is there for you to make a selection.
It serves creativity, individuality, and free will.
And there is enough for all.
"Enough" was created by God –
Enough for all.
God does not select, favor, or hold back.
The story of Adam and Eve (and it is a story)
Could also be the story of the corruption, but not destruction,

Of God's perfect plan of love.
The garden is that plan which God had for its creation.
Everything was there to be selected and enjoyed.
There was no idea that there would be difficulty, or that there would
	not be enough.
The belief in unworthiness served as confirmation of the belief in
	separation.
Lucky and unlucky, good and bad –
These also served the belief in separation.
The voice of God that Adam and Eve heard,
Ordering them form the garden,
Was their own ego's voice
That they thought was God's voice
Ordering them from their place of love.
You have never been expelled from God's love.
You can never be separate from it or undeserving of it.
God never created another place for you to go, where there was no love.
There is only what you have created, believing this is so.
The belief in scarcity and separation is the nightmare you dream
And your manifestations can reflect that nightmare.
What the world and your ego tell you
Is idealistic… unobtainable… too good to be true,
Actually IS true.

The garden exists forever and you are in it
As you rid yourself of false intent and fears,
You will hear the true voice of God saying,
"What do you want?"
"Select… partake… enjoy."

⊷══◎══⊷

The purest expression of love
(closest to God's love)
Is unconditional love.
It takes time to develop and understand this love.
But it is love totally gratifying
And free of fear.
The treasure of love
Is not just in "having it."
But how you feel,
As you give it and receive it.

From the Creator

It is not about progress,
But about you
That I wish to speak.
Since your beginning,
I have looked at you… loving you… loving that part of me.
I have never lost sight of you. Not one second of any lifetime.
Wearing garments of shadow or garments of light –
You have stayed in front of my eyes.
And what I see, I love
And love and love.
When you are through with the ego,
Which there is no doubt you will be,
You will come to know yourself and be free…
At first, you will think you are experiencing me –
As though we could ever stand apart.
You will experience you and me and US.
Knowing yourself and being yourself
Will be your progress.
It will also be your joy and mine.
You do not know that your nature is mine.
You were MY miracle.
Knowing and being yourself will be yours.
You do not know the difference you make. I do.
What you do in this lifetime
You do for yourself
And for me.
Into your hand, I will place another's hand
And you will know partnership.

It will be you and another
And, through that,
…you and me…

I see you – what you do and who you are.
What I see, I love.
And I love, and I love, and I continue to love.

Printed in the USA
CPSIA information can be obtained
at www.ICGtesting.com
LVHW040619050324
773470LV00001B/38